SUNDRIES

Collected poems of Mitchell Forrest Lyman

CHAPEL HILL
PRESS, INC.

ISBN 1-880849-82-8
Library of Congress Catalog Number 2004100291

Printed in the United States of America
First Printing

Contents

Foreword

There are times when I wonder if Gutenberg, when he invented a printing press, really did me a favor, since I find it hard to ignore anything in print. Even before I started school I was learning words from comic strips: BIFF, BAM, PSST, EEK, and the longer HARUMPH. I was early hooked on reading, which led me to pursue English as my college major. Poetry was the genre that appealed to me most. When an English professor introduced the class to Edward Fitzgerald's translation of *The Rubaiyat of Omar Khayyam*, the hook sank deeper, and has never been removed.

Thirty years went by before I had the leisure and the impulse to concentrate on writing poems. It was then, in about 1970, that I co-founded a group that came to be called The Friday Noon poets, freely open to any interested persons. In 1979 this group assembled an anthology, *Poetry Under the Stars*. In 1995 I put together a 62-page book of my poems titled *Kaleidoscope*. In this volume, titled *Sundries*, are assembled choices from the previous publications, plus a number of new poems.

I have striven to stay within these guidelines: "Literate, but stuffy; insightful, but not pedantic; tough and honest, but not sen tional." If you should use my combinations of words, please credit authorship, and spell my name right. Thanks.

Dear Readers, my strongest wish is to share these poems with y hoping they may illuminate your own experiences.

Stub Of A Pencil

When failing to reverse the earth,
One's impotence produces rage,
There's a therapeutic worth
In scribbling on the page.

—Mitchell Forrest Lyman, in her 85th year

Acknowledgments

I hereby record my sincere thanks for any person who may have praised my poetry, and any publication which has included them. You know who you are.

Accountability

Numbers have a will of their own—
Vicious little beats—
Cutting up—Cutting out—
Disappearing when I need them most;
Not staying in straight lines,
Seldom giving correct answers,
Outwitting me on every page,
Creeping in and out of my musings,
Starring in my nightmares,
Keeping me continually off balance—

Ah, balance! There's the key word.
Pile them on the scales opposite truth—
They lie so much!!

Appearances Deceive

When I am powdered
    and bedangled,

Then you may know
    my life is tangled;

But if my shirttail's out
    and my nose is shiny,

Then you should know
    my cares are tiny!

If Only

Far down the road a car
    approached;

I knew it was bringing my
    dearest friends,

So I leaped up, and ran to
    meet them—

Anything is possible
    in dreams.

As Beautiful As Words

Some things are just plain beautiful
    so that the greatest artist in the world
        could not improve on nature.

    A peacock's fan spread out and shimmering;
    A deer's delicate hoof tapping the ground;
    A dove's iridescence trembling at sight of mate;
    A baby focusing on his first Christmas tree—

These are the headline events,
    but just as miraculous is the sprouting of seeds,
        knowing exactly what they are to be:

A coconut, wave-bounced to an alien shore,
    splitting its thick husk, and forcing its sprouts
        into the sand;

Pines and cedars springing unbidden
    over scars along the Interstates;

A salmon braving the falls reversely;
Eggs hatching true to their genes;
A literate adult guiding a juvenile finger
    over the lines in a reading manual;

continued

His hand touching the nape of her neck,
   causing her to turn fully towards him—

More beautiful than words.

Wedding Anniversary

From disparate trees did our planks come
   to form a durable shelter,
With stresses plied for strength,
Edges smoothed with sand and oil,
Pattern laid on in light and dark,
   and beads of pearl—

Like mortise and tenon are we joined.

Bar Scene

Remembering flesh
    against flesh,

Cells crawl
    along the brass rail,

Vibrate to the brushes
    of the drummer,

Slide along the reach
    to nowhere.

Hideaway

There is motion in stillness;
There is sound in silence.

Lightning gave us fire;
Thunder gave us fear.

Every day we may be only a millimeter,
Or a second short of earthquake.

Ready the storm cellar;
We must have a hideaway.

Blessed Balm

We met at the fabric shop,
You buying remnants of velvet
    to frame your thoughts-in-oil,
I looking for thread to let down
    last year's hem—

Your glance framed my feelings,
Your touch rubbed smooth a lump,
Your words stitched up a wound—

O, salve,
O, ointment,
O, blessed balm of friendship.

Blossoming

It approaches minute by minute the hour
When incipient blossoms shall flower—

O, holy, holy, holy,
I am most wholly involved—

I care that Spring shall again erupt
So that our spirits, bankrupt
From winter's harsh withdrawals,
Shall have the cash deposits
Of love, hope, commiseration,
And all knowledge true
Shall flow between me and you—

Happy, O, most glorious springtime,
Rise up in us all!

NOTE: For the musical setting of this poem, please see the Appendix

Breakfast Blessing, As Incanted by "Pop"

It seemed to me, a ten-year-old girlchild, that the day could not officially begin until he sat enthroned at the head of the large table, with the bountiful food spread out, steam rising from the mound of sausage, scrambled eggs, and hash brown potatoes, first seared in a deep iron skillet, then moistened with milk while they finished cooking in the oven where the cornbread baked.

He began the first words, "O, Lord," in a deep roar that bounced off the ceiling, and bombarded my half-asleep eardrums, lowered over the waiting plate.

He would continue the litany in a rumble, "make us grateful for these, and all blessings that pour down on us from heaven above. Amen" —the last word dwindling to a whisper, the whole delivery having been done in one breath, bellowing out from the barrel chest.

There were times when my empty stomach would also rumble, to my threatened embarrassment; but I don't think he ever heard it, so intent was he on talking to God.

Now, I had walked the cornfield where had grown the grain to make the bread; and I had weeded the potato patch; I had petted the pig now ground into sausage; I had fed the hens and gathered the eggs. At no time did I see any of this provender fall from heaven.

I was confused.

Clocks

Clocks come in multifarious designs,
     materials, and sizes.

To view compelling evidence, visit
     The Clock Museum at The Smithsonian.

Consider how timepieces are arbitrary,
     alarming, and dictatorial;

Even though they may gain, or lose a little,
     they compel us to arrive, or depart
          at a certain moment, whether we
               feel ready, or not.

Do not offend with lateness; neither arrive
     before the appointed second.

Sort out your options, if any:

Is this a one-time-only event, never
     to be duplicated?

Will there be a later train, plane, or bus?

Oh, come on! Read History!!

The Color Red

Several years into widowhood, there was one year
    when I didn't buy any clothing
        that wasn't *red*—
            including panties and petticoats—

Mercy me!
    and shades of Scarlett O'Hara—
        and Rhett Butler, who is quoted as saying,
            "Frankly, my dear, I don't give a damn!"

And that was sad. pitifully *sad*,
    because they really *loved* each other;
But there was all that *stress*
    due to the War Between The States,
And the great *burden* that was put on *Scarlett*
    to save the pious, and ever-forgiving *Melanie*—

    and *Ashley's baby*

        from the ravaged Atlanta—

Christ on a crutch!

How did we ever *save Atlanta*?

Daybreak

Blue morning slides
    through the evergreens,
        through the pink of my gown,
           and shafts me with sunbeams

Midnight

The world is lovely then,
Smooth and deep;
Turning softly,
Murmuring in sleep.

Spiders venture from their webs,
Crickets endlessly tune;
It is then that I endlessly search
For the there, unbreakable rune.

Time Burns

Time burns swiftly, and is consumed
    on the grate of experience.
Sift hard diamonds from the ashes,
    and with the residue grow sturdy oaks.

England's Royals

The royal family is like cathedrals,
    long time abuilding,
expensive to maintain,
        but dazzling.
Observe the Queen—how stately,
        how resplendent—
Arched timbers, jewelled windows,
        buttressed by lesser titles,
        epochs in every line—
Royal purple over red carpet—
        history's promenade.

Predictability/Variability

No one can dictate to anyone the age they are,
nor can we forecast the experiences someone will have,
and certainly not exactly how they will react.

Sociologists spend endless hours, and reams of paper
analyzing what has happened in populations, and
what next is likely to occur.

Fortunes rise and fall on their reports.

Exploring My Purse

Let's get to the bottom of this gulch;
It's becoming like layers of mulch—

A piece of gum that sticks to the fingers;
A vial of perfume whose fragrance lingers;

An ad for a movie called *Center Stage*—
Wonder why it was all the rage?

Here's another, imported from France:
Croupier—Is that a roulette dance?

Some Traveler's Checks I haven't spent
For a trip to Ireland, where I never went.

Should I have focused on *Saving Grace,*
Though in my purse it has no place?

I'm at the bottom now—Call it a day;
Thomas the Magic Railroad, take it away!

Family

I remember saying to a daughter-in-law,
    over the long-distance telephone,

I love you, and I love my sons, both of them,
    beyond the point of definable description;

And I know that each of them is a wonderful
    person, though certainly not identical,
        and not expected to be "perfect";

Since no one can more than roughly predict
    what any fetus will be like,

With its generations of proclivities,
    and potentialities only suspected,

I felt that my job—beyond loving them—
    was to fully nurture them, praise
        them, and reward them at home,

Hoping that as they eased into the adult
    world, their behavior would be such as
        to be rewarded outside the family circle.

The sweetest praise may be that from an
    unrelated person about one of your own.

Here's a vivid allegory: One stick alone is easy
    to break, but a bundle of sticks held together
        is very hard to break—

That's family!

The Next Step

This first-born son, who threatened to fall
    early from the womb,
Now struggles to free himself from home.
    Hunched over a book,
        ears closed to family,
    Knees drawn up, he continues
        his nativity.
Awash in hi-fi sound, he's shielded
    from a hostile world,
And from square corners of parents
    abrasive to his soul.

Fear For The Gentle

Fear for the gentle of the earth
For they shall be flattened
Under the caterpillar treads;
And they shall carpet the earth
In shades of blood-red and yellow,
For they lack conviction
To spring back, upright,
From the mower's blade.

Sometimes

Sometimes when you are trying to sort the this and the that,
Sometimes life hits you over the head like a baseball bat.

Sometimes life swamps you like a flash flood, or tidal wave,
And you wonder if you can somehow rebuild before the grave.

When life unfolds before you, dragging what's behind you,
You hope that a modicum of success will somehow find you.

Did anybody ever tell you that Life would be one long Ball?
O, come on, listen up, look around, and evaluate, you all.

For Susjanti, From Bali, Learning English

Teacher:
Would you care
To see a bear?

Perhaps a deer?
Beware, my dear

If go you would
Through the wood,

Bend a bough
And see a cow;

Or in terror
Fall in a burrow;

Would you want
A house to haunt?

To live beguiled
In the wild?

Susjanti:
That's enough—
It's too tough!

Fur-lined Roadway

Wheel-flattened squirrel
    on the macadam,
Only the fuzzy tail
    still waving
        contentiously—

Human's Best Friend
(or How to Deal with Dogs)

From roaming the vast outdoors, and a far rough,
They were first of the wild to come in to the hearth,

Where they found a warm, dry curl-up space,
For dreaming dreams that time can't erase.

Bringing down the game is what they can do;
Their reward is a pat, and their name in the stew.

'Gather ye rosebuds while ye may,
old time is still a-flying;
and this same flower that smiles today,
tomorrow will be dying.'

—ROBERT HERRICK (1591-1674)

Growing Good Things

I plant a petunia,
And a marigold,
Thinking young,
Though I am old.
And when the blooms
Wither, fade, and fall,
I ponder if perhaps
That may be all.

Then chide myself
For thinking thus—
Growing good things
Is always a plus.

Haiku/Loku

When I encountered the genre of poetry called Haiku, I thought there was only one form; that is, a three-line poem with five syllables in the first line, seven in the second, and five in the third, without rhyme, or complete sentences, but with reference to nature. When I had an idea which I thought might be good for this genre, and then I couldn't fit it in the 5-7-5 frame, I invented a word, "Loku," for a poem which is short, but not as condensed as seventeen syllables.

Here is my example of a Loku:

Discard

Dry leaves in corners of steps
    whirled by winter's winds—
        old thoughts beyond their usefulness,
            outworn premises to be swept away.

And here it is condensed into the 5-7-5 syllabication:

Whirled by winter's winds
Dry leaves in corners of steps
Worn thoughts swept away

I should say that I have recently read a 350-page book on the history of Haiku which points out that the Haiku genre has gone through a number of lengths, syllabications, and subjects acceptable in their time, so I may have written more Haiku than I know. However, I have a strong feeling that only in the Japanese language can we find true haiku.

Hard As Nails

After so much talk,
    so much silence.

The talk was needed,
    that's for sure;

That much talk,
    and so much more.

The silence is more violent,
    more punishing and cruel;

I think I'd prefer the gruel
    of all that yammering

To this hard silence
    hammering, hammering
    at my door.

Hate Kills

He hugged his hurts to his chest,
Gathered his grievances like plaque,
Stuffed his arteries with fatted wrongs
    until his carotid split wide open,

And death leaped in.

Now Let Us Bury Dead Love

Remove the roses,
    the gladiolus;
Throw off the fading
    forget-me-nots,
Cruel rebukers
    of present thoughts.
Pile on the weeds,
    the dry seed heads,
        even the briars.
Cease the wailing,
    dry the eyes,
        ignite this pyre;
The time has come to
    murmur the prayer
        for the dead.

Healing

How can we heal the hurt?
How reduce the damage?
How clean up the mess
Resulting from the carnage?

Every battle that is fought,
If it be scrimmage, or war,
Leaves parts that are broken,
And many a long, livid scar.

When the troops withdraw,
And bivouac for the night,
Will they ask themselves,
"Is the battle worth the fight?"

How Babies Are Made

Sometimes only with lust;
Sometimes only with passion;
But the best way is with love,
    and tender care,
Followed by joyous anticipation,
    overlying nausea,
        fatigue, worry,
            and the unbalanced budget;

Then the hardest work,
    termed labor,
        releasing into the breathing world
A new, unique, and never-to-be-
        exactly-duplicated,
            real, live person.

A baby should be made
    with tender, loving care.

Hunger

Food is absolutely vital,
  whether it be elaborate gourmet,
    or a fruit picked from its tree.

In any dwelling the kitchen's the core.

People can survive without food
  longer than without water;

Dessication is a painful state, and
  starvation is terminal—

Witness the sight of African children
  who have not had a full meal in months,
    muscles shrinking as bellies distend,
      eyes receding into taut skulls—

There is no supermarket within their reach.

In Olden Days

My grandparents had horses and mules,
Walked behind the plow, and other tools;

Gee, Haw, at least six days a week,
Kept them strong, and seldom weak;

Whoa; unhitch; went then to the feed,
Knowing what the stock would need:

A meadow thick with lush green grass,
And when the summer season was past,

The loft of barn was stuffed with hay,
To be pitchforked down day after day

When in winter they'd be long in their stall;
And the folks, far from any shopping mall,

Were enjoying their bounty of strawberry jam,
Dried beans, peas, apples, and smoked ham;

Biscuits, corn bread, and cake from the grain
They had grown with their might and main,

Along with potatoes, both white and yellow,
Stored with pumpkins in the root cellar.

continued

Poultry were fed, and their eggs were stored
In baskets 'til there was a sufficient hoard

For the ladies to hie off to the general store
To buy sugar, salt, cloth, thread, and more—

Only things they could not grow themselves,
To be carefully stored at home on the shelves,

Then measured out as needed, and tasted
So not one ounce or one inch would be wasted;

Careful they were, conserving in all ways—
And that's how it was in The Olden Days.

Interstate Truck Traffic

Lumbering elephants,
    trunk to tail,
        trunk to tail,
            trunk to tail,

Rumbling deep in their throats
    their warnings,
        and exhortations,

Trumpeting travel hints:
    How far to the water hole
        with the greenest thorn trees,
            the nearest pit stop for the herd.

Are the children keeping up?
    Only the mothers know.

It's Hard To Be Different Before 11 P.M.

Say, did you ever stay up all night,
   having pretended to turn in
      with the rest of the family?

But your churning mind was too noisy for sleep,

So you wandered the house—from kitchen—
   to bath—to basement—
And finally parked in the STUDY,

Where you might have *studied*,
   had there not been a mirror on the wall,
      bevel-edged, and all,

Which put you in a traffic rotary,
   when what you really wanted was OUT—
A wide EXIT to a new town
   where the charter allows
      particularity—

Like, say, if you want to raise chickens
    in your backyard,
And I want to practice the flute,
We're free to try to
    synchronize—

And wouldn't that be lovely, and all-wise,
Your cock crowing well on his heap o' dung,
And I rejoicing with loud flute notes,
    sincerely flung!

Invasions

The dirt under my fingernails
    is from printer's ink,
Transitory thoughts rubbed off
    in the handling.

Used to be, in my gardening years,
    real alluvial soil; that is,
When I lived in the lowlands
    between two rivers.

Now that I've settled on a
    rocky ridge in Zone 7,
Gardening is a hardship case,
    with results uncertain.

Still, I pore over the nursery catalogs,
    sucking in the beauty of each illustration,
Studying the fine print, and making long
    lists as to suitability:

There's full sun, or partial shade;
    soil that's acid, or alkaline;
There's annual, or perennial (I hope);
    climbing, or not; invasive or non-invasive.

I frowningly survey my clay-bound
    rocky hillside, and pray,
"O, in green, or brilliant color, please,
    Mother/Father Nature, INVADE ME!"

It's Love

It's Love
When you want him to use the best fishing rod,
and the reel which does not snarl the nylon line;
and you want him to catch not only the first,
but the biggest fish of the day;

It's Love
when he gives you for Mother's Day
the most exotic hand-tied lure;

It's Love
When he hands you the bait bucket,
and himself hoists the outboard motor;

It's Love
When he puts the bloodworms on your hook,
and you know he'll remove the snagged fish
without being asked;

It's Love
When you are heating the cast iron skillet,
he's cleaning the catch—except for the biggest,
which you will have mounted for Father's Day,

With Love.

Jigsaw Puzzle, Pieces Missing

Like you, I have shed many tears;
Choked on the dust, and despaired
    of finding life;
Grieved with the families and friends
    left behind who will never find even
        the part of a body over which to moan—
Death without closure—

I see in my mind's eye again and again
    the picture of the helmeted firemen
        raising the Stars and Stripes,
And I think that photograph will live in history
    and art and sculpture as the photo from WW II
        of the soldiers raising the American Flag
            at Iwo Jima—a turning point in the struggle
                of freedom versus repression.

I regret to say that I sometimes view my life as
    "one damned war after another"—

And now we know that men have found a new way
    to kill thousands of people at once,

        another milestone in history.

        DAMN!

Kaleidoscope

We gather our data
    bit by bit:

    A followed by B,
    1 succeeded by 2,
        or fractions thereof,
           and so forth—

But it's never so measured,
    nor so consistent—
There are leaps to peaks,
And fall backs into abysses.

From the caverns of the house
    voices rise:

    They whisper,
    They recant,
    They propose
        in alternating tones,
           the sound track
               for the moving picture.

We add the multicolored fragments
    piece by piece,

        the gems and the gravels
            side by each,

And twirl them into
    scene after scene.

Kite Fights At Emerald Isle

The bat kite lurches higher and higher into azure sky;

The kite like a jellyfish chases the bat, its poisonous
    tentacles closing in for the kill;

A merciful gust flips the bat out of reach;

Quickly comes a snake insinuating its pointed head
    into the fray;

Beachcombers point upward;

Small children see only bright bobbing colors at the ends
    of long strings held by their parents, their bodies moving
        in mild mockery, relishing the game;

I am reminded of Spitfires and Messerschmitts dogfighting
    above the cliffs of Dover.

Last Rights

I pray thee, that when I am done,
Do not through tubes allow to run
Synthetic sense when I have none.

Whatever then is left of me
Should go to fertilize a tree
Whose form would be my history:

Roots that are deep in America
Both near to origin, and far,
Since distance has not been a bar

To where the heart may lodge its care;
There'd be new buds every year
And, it is hoped, new fruit to bear.

Leaving

The children left today,
    slipping away at sunrise.

    I lay abed, only my heartbeat rising;
We had said our goodbyes the night before,
        after a feast in The Dragon's Garden,

      hands gripping shoulders,
        cheeks brushing,

      eyes hungry as camera shutters,
        snapping clear pictures
          to look at

        even in the dark.

Levity

A little bit of levity lightens the load,
Even if under the stone there's a toad;
Though he appears to be asleep,
He's gathering strength for a leap.

Leaping is what he does best;
And that's a message for the rest:
Find your dearest proclivity,
And go for it with a little levity.

Parlaying

Parlay the patchwork to the penultimate;
Don't waste time arguing the course of Fate;
Don't take cruel punishment lying down;
Switch quickly to a smile from a frown;
As to where, when, and why, analyze, analyze;
Preferably, our bad luck should be another guy's!

Lightning

How often does lightning strike a person, or thing?
Oh, far too often for anyone within its range.

I saw a documentary on The Public Broadcasting System
   which claimed that lightning strikes from the ground up.

Really? Well, it happens too fast for me to tell, but if it
   does, then it's The Great Deceiver.

What I can confirm is that the thunder comes later, right
   after the blinding flash and the sulphurous odor.

Observe the huge trees split asunder, chimneys knocked
   off their bases, houses in ashes, bodies scarred forever.

There are tales, sworn to be true, of balls of fire rolling
   through an open window, and leaving out the back door.

I, myself, when a child, was sitting in a dining room when
   lightning came along the telephone wires, rang the phone
      on the wall, jangled the water glasses full for supper.

Another storm, when my father was driving the tractor to
the barn, veered too close to a wire fence, from which
that unholy fire leaped to his tractor, and gave him a
mighty jolt. He was one of the lucky ones—he lived
to tell the tale.

There are people who welcome an electrical storm, beam at
the turbulent sky, and say, "How beautiful!"

But I am not one of the admirers; to me, it is awful. I close
the draperies, and huddle on the sofa with my trembling
dog, surrounded by trees taller than my sanctuary.

I figure the tallest tree will take the charge.

Magnifiers

Slipping the convex glass with its steel bezel,
    and looped handle

From its frayed canvas case, as its previous owner,
    my husband, had done for many years,

I recall his hand moving the glass over the details
    of the drawing of a ship, checking its rigging,
        its masts, planking, anchor, figurehead,
            flags, and pennants, and the stance of
            the captain at the wheel,

Under his glass all greatly enlarged.

He, too, was bigger than life,
    and too soon diminished.

Mean Encounter

The weighted glance,
    the dismissing hand,

The indrawn breath,
    the upthrust stand;

The hasty departure,
    no backward glance,

And all because he
    must lead the dance.

Memorable Treads

Haven't you noticed how each person has a distinctive,
    recognizable pattern of walking,
        of putting one foot in front of the other, making tracks,
Be it over bare, or lushly carpeted floor,
    over hard, echoing concrete,
        or rough, unleveled ground,
So that you can say to yourself,
    "Oh, that's Margie, my neighbor;
        or it's the monthly meter reader."
Or it can be yourself moving painfully, albeit joyously,
    to answer the insistent peal of the doorbell.
Just so does each creature have a characteristic pattern
    of propelling itself from Point A to Point B.
Take, for instance, my little devil of a dog:
    How well I know the click, click of his four feet,
        toenails tapping their tattoo,
          through my house,
            through my brain.

Messages

The clock goes ticktock, ticktock;
The heart goes flubub, flubub;
The foot goes pattey, tepatty, pat;

The cricket goes chirrp, chirrp;
The cardinal goes twut, twuttwut;
And what do you think of that?

Sounds are a kind of language,
Of that I have no doubt;
When my dog says woof, woof,
I usually know what it's about.

There's a different woof for hunger,
Or boredom, or needing to go out;
And if I don't heed the message,
You may be sure he'll pout.

He might even soil the rug,
Then hide out under the bed;
But that's always because
The message was not really read.

Milk And Honey

My love pours over you
    like milk from a pitcher,
        thick with cream,
Anointing your body
    from the tips of your black hair
        to the white edge of your toenails,
           curling with delight;

Place your lips here—
    drink deep, and know
        it is the river that runs
           through Paradise.

Enough Love

You asked me once in later years,
    "How much is enough?"

And I could not answer,
    knowing that sometimes

There is enough love
    in the touch of a fingertip.

Mirrored Eye

On the way to church this morning
    my wagon wheel crushed
        a little bird,
            smaller even than most.

How could this have happened?
    If I'd been trying,
        I couldn't have hit it.

Always before, birds
    have swerved away
        in that life-saving lift,
            so swift, so enviable.

Now I hear that thump
    in every pothole,

See that eye
    in every mirror.

Muddy River—Day

The thick brown river,
now straight, now bowed,
serpentines through green marsh,
its sides scored by
stiff cattails.

This round brown body,
now hissing, now gurgling,
sluggishly gathering
on its rough underbelly
countless particles of
upland soil, brown gold,
roils on to low-lying
wetlands.

Muddy River—Snowstorm

In the downfall flail
of hoary blizzard
the serpent's back is pocked
by snowflakes.

All wildfowl fall silent.
Mink and muskrat huddle
in their straw houses.
Frogs are mute in mud banks.
Ice shards cling to cattails,
And no fish dares to break
through the skim.

Muddy River—Night

In the deep shade
Of a moonless landscape
The sepia serpent's tongue
Searches for prey to
Swallow whole.

Natural Colors

Green is one of my favorite colors;
It ranks way up there
    with sunshine yellow,
        and sky blue.

Without the blue and yellow,
    no way we could have the green—

And let's include the colorless rain,
    dropping through the yellow and blue,

To cause the green to grow.

I'll spread my composted garbage,
    plant my packet of wildflower seeds,

And trust I'll be rewarded with a rainbow!

No No, Woodrow

Please do not piddle on the parsley;
Parsley is for people in the house;
I would like to use it in my soup
Without detergent for a douse.

Can't you make it to the nearest oak?
Or, better yet, the compost pile?
That's the perfect place, I think;
Then I could greet you with a smile.

Really, Woodrow, patience wears thin;
Your shenanigans increasingly pall;
If you fail Diane's Obedience Class,
The Taxidermist may be my next call.

Stop playing me for the sucker
you know me to be;
Eternal vigilance is the price
of your liberty.

Partners

A hand has five fingers,
The mind has one;
A foot has five toes,
But cannot run
Unless it's partnered
With the other one.

So must the body and the soul
Perform always a double role,
Not entering the stage of life
Unless it be as man and wife—

Two entities commingled as one;
And so together the play is run.

Precious Rain

Ever so gently did it come down,
No pitter-patter on the ground;

There it soaked slowly in
Where reaching roots begin

To claim their share of turf;
And Mother Nature allots the worth

Of this claim, or possibly those,
As to which shrivels, which grows;

Without water, none can live,
So, precious rain, give, give, give!

So Weeps the Rain

Some think it represents the planet's pain;
Others resent its wetness, and complain;
I worry it may not come again—
Now, tonight, so weeps the rain!

Primary Physician

He came in the middle of the night
    to give his expert opinion
So my beloved could be legally
    carried to the crematorium.

As I said goodnight to our doctor
    outside the front door,
I briefly touched his shoulder
    with my forehead, and said,

"Thank you for making a house call
    in the middle of the night."

Reciprocity

Like relentlessly burrowing earthworms,
There are thoughts which make inroads
in my brain.

I cannot every day answer why.

Mother Nature's laws, though forever
modifying, are inescapable,

Whether you are an ape, or a humanoid,
a beaver, a bird, or an insect;

How marvelous to see birds flitting
through a grove of trees,
plucking insects as they go;

To see a woodpecker working
a worm-infested tree,
top to bottom.

Observe closely the small birds
who ride the backs of hippopotami,
feeding on the vermin
which infest them.

continued

Note the beaver damming its winter cache;

The squirrel burying acorns
which in spring will sprout;

The housewife carrying a casserole
to her grieving neighbor—

The word "reciprocity" comes to mind.

A Ride In The Tow Truck

It was an emergency, sort of
Though not one I'd thought of

In just that particular way:
Getting from Point B to A:

A medical appointment at an hour early,
After hours of fasting, making me surly;

And from real hunger, faint—
Something I usually ain't.

When I staggered to my car,
I thought, "Oh, my, it's too far

To the doctor's chair;
I just can't make it there!"

Then I had the best of luck:
My grandson came in his tow truck.

He said, "Get in the truck; I'll tow your car,
And deliver you both to the Clinic, not far."

continued

When we arrived, my doctor was just reporting;
He looked astonished at my transporting,

But graciously helped me down,
And escorted me in without a frown.

When I was done with the annual "oughta,"
There in the parking lot was my little auto,

Parked exactly between the lines, white,
So I drove it home, feeling just right.

Serendipity is just the proper name,
And serendipitous is that grandson's fame.

Room for a Different Opinion

This do I know full well and more:
Older people bemoan and deplore;

Socrates was accused of youth corrupting,
And I, for one, am often interrupting

A contrary view from someone not old—
Shouldn't I praise them for being bold?

How could I think the world according to me
Is exactly how the world ought to be?!

A Row of Dogwoods

Behold their dazzling whiteness,
    the perfect quadriform of their bracts,
        each tipped with a splash of red;

Some say it represents the blood of Christ
    on the cross, a fanciful metaphor.

That row along the curb reminds me of my husband
    who planted them, some from seed gathered on
        the Chapel Hill campus, thirty years ago.

Glad I am he lived to see them bloom; sorry I am
    he died, in the Fall of '77, just when our dogwoods
        were dropping their round red seeds.

Ever since, I tend that row of Cornus Florida Alba,
    and the one "sport" Rubra, as a memorial to him,
        and a beauteous sight to the neighborhood.

Sail Ho

Hungering for the enticing horizon,
    through eons, men have set out
        on the bounding main,

Breathing deeply
    the salt-laden air.

Round that buoy, helmsman;
    tack home;

Penelope has prepared your dinner,
    and soon will brush down
        her long golden hair.

Sames and Differences

The psyche and the soma
Sleep in the same bed,
Bathe in the same water,
Dine at the same table,
Eating the same menu.

How they metabolize,
And with what results,
That's where they diverge:
A fatty deposit here,
A slender poem there—

But horse and rider as one—

What a wonderful ride on the carousel!

The Second Season

Cicadas saw in contrapuntal rhythm
    as sprinklers arc over lilac and leaves,
        and trickles of water snake underground.

Flashes of firefly yellow belie caution—
    guitar notes fall in casual caress—

A cyclist's arabesques on the macadam
    draw from a nubile girl loud applause,
And dogs from house to house are startled
    into anxious dialogue.

The cyclist's older brother, with one-armed aplomb,
    wheels his rod around the corner,
        blending exhaust with sweet petunia
            and acrid marigold.

The housebound Burmese cat peers from the crossbeam
    into the wooded darkness beyond her wall of glass;

And you and I move out to the hammock
    under the dogwood canopy.

Beside the August-green poinsettia
    we sway in humid air,
        framed in moonbeams,
            bracketed by time—
                easing through the second season.

Shades of Meaning

Truth comes clothed in varied garbs;
Hand-me-downs are what rumors wear;

Falsehood shades its eyes with many masks,
While candor's coat is always clear.

Now when I go out along the streets,
It's rainbow colors I parade in;

But when I meet a friend of true insight,
It's Eve's undress that I'm arrayed in!

Feelings Are Facts

It's good to have a friend, a fact,
To talk things over before you act;

Or even if you have already acted,
And the results have heavily impacted

On these, and them, and others—
All your sisters and your brothers—

So you're wringing your hands, saying, "Drat!"
Yes, it's great to have a caring ear, a fact.

Shadows

The way the shadows move
    about this house
makes the blood surge,

Shifting in diurnal patterns,
    east to west,
and as the seasons merge;

The chorus line of leaves,
    the bare branches,
dancing down the hall—

Sometimes it seems
    it's *your* shadow
thrust against the wall.

Sounds In An Empty House

The dialogue is between
    furnace and refrigerator,
        set against each other:
            heat against cold—

Stressful joints creak
    as pines sough by roof,
        and embers grow grey—

Listen!

Could that be a key in the lock?
    A hand upon the door?

Stockpiling

By the window sewing buttons against the cold,
The corner of her eye catches a plump squirrel
Stowing nuts to last the winter's span.

In the panelled room under the rug by the hearth
The family dog tucks a gnawed beef knuckle
Stealthily, as her ancestors must have saved
Against the hunt when no prey would fall.

Hauling groceries another day the housewife,
With something extra in case of storm,
Passes the Andrews Arsenal, and feels
Herself cringe and quiver as soldiers
Tuck the warheads gently underground.

The Surf

And there is the surf,
   crashing again and again
     against the edge of land,
The moon taking it out,
   and bringing it back again,
    lower, and higher,
      lower, and higher,
        again, and again,
         never ceasing,
          never ceasing,
            never ceasing—

And what time o'tide shall we walk the sandy shore?
And shall we wear shoes against sharp and empty shells?
Or no shoes so as to sink our toes in the malleable sand?

Either way, it's primitive and vital to touch base again
               with our beginnings.

Time After Time

On the Gregorian Calendar
Time comes round in twelve segments,
Predictable as any time can be.

Time has not only nanoseconds,
But epochs and eons.

It has flashes of illumination,
Long-held secrets revealed.

Time can rush by in frivolous games,
Or it can creep in measures of grief.

You cannot stop the pendulum;
Nor can you hurry a minute into an hour.

Time cannot be avoided, or bypassed.
Synchronize your timepieces.

Time is always before you, and behind you;
To ignore it incurs a penalty.

Waiting is hard, even for a flower to bloom,
Or an egg to hatch.

To A Traveling Husband

Here on the pillow the musk
    of you clings;
When will the all
    of you return?

I hold this remnant,
    and wait
To be wrapped again
    in the whole cloth.

Quarrel

We are with each other as brittle
    as yesterday's toast.
Your irascible crust
    scratches my eardrums—

Silently across the table
    I implore:
Butter me with soft words, Beloved,
    or I crumble.

To A Warm Friend

If there were a crevice
        to the cavern of your chest,
I would slip inside,
        and never again be cold.

Widow

She holds herself
        like a cracked egg—
                rigidly erect—
so the body inside
                does not spill out.

To My Belly Dance Teachers

You are water rushing over rocks;
>You are pines bending in the wind;
>>You are sunlight breaking through fog;
>>>You are fireflies flickering at dusk—

You are weather, going from calm to storm,
>and back again to calm—

You are poetry in motion.

Traumas

The cracked tile,
The chipped plate,
The cup, nicked
>just where the lips press
>>to sip the flow—

There's leakage there—

And also where
>the abraded heart
>>oozes at the shut door.

To My Mother, 1897-1989

See how that lonely flower,
    the bloom past gone,
        droops its head;

Hear the doctors say,
    after long years of care,
        not just wilted—dead;

Bring forth the memories
    of when the rose still blushed,
        and the root still fed.

Toss-Away Day

Someday we must clean out this cupboard—
    someday soon we'll organize,
        like on a Wednesday, because
            the trash man comes on Thursday—

We'll make a mound of our debris:
    The dreams that never fit the frame;
    The hopes that spoiled in storage;
    The ugly words that cracked in quarrels;
    The days we wasted in good intentions—

        And all the years not good enough to save.

Traveling Words

People seen talking to themselves
Are considered dottery;
Maybe they're just mentally molding
A piece of pottery;

Or hurling imprecations and curses
At those addicted to doggerel verses;

Even so, I'll try not to talk aloud
When mingling with a crowd;

Words can hurl, words can sift;
Words can target, words can drift;

What I aim for them to do
Is to travel 'til they reach you.

Until It Rises

I can't write a poem until it rises,
Coming to me in many guises,
Whether as a rainbow after a storm,
Or a tornado flattening a barn—

O, a nearby asylum I hope to find
'Cause Gaia isn't always kind.

Available Art

That conch hollowed by the sea,
A sculpture Picasso might have done;

Take note of the pretty petunia,
Glowing as Matisse's brushed one;

And there a cardinal zipping by
Puts Chagall's doves on the run—

All nature is a gallery of art
Available to everyone.

Up Early

Not reading the calendar,
Nor phases of the moon,
Crocuses push up from earth,
    And bloom, bloom, bloom.

Words as Knives

    Poets are like surgeons—
    We use words like scalpels
    To probe the psyche
    Of the universe,
    Lance the festering spot,
    Then clamp the bleeding wound.

The Waiting Room

The appointment's at ten;
I arrive one minute before,
Knowing doctors, mostly men,
Laggard patients deplore.

He's already running slow;
The nurse shrugs her regrets;
I settle by the reading lamp's glow
Beside one ahead, who also frets.

I pick up last year's GEOGRAPHIC,
Peruse the mating habits of snakes;
Judge it only mildly pornographic,
Really only just what it takes.

As one by one she leads us away,
The nurse now smiles at our gloom
As we bid farewell later that day
To space so aptly named The Waiting Room.

The Wall on the Mall

Not just on the Federally-designated Memorial Day,
But on any, and every day of the year, in all weathers,
People of all ages come to The Wall, dark and dense,
    on the District of Columbia Mall,

To search for the names of comrades, and relatives
    who gave up their lives in that ill-begotten Asian War.

Be they buddies or families of the memorialized,
    they trace the name with their forefinger, often lean
        their foreheads against the cold stone, wash it with
            tears, wipe it with their clean handkerchiefs,

Then take a rubbing of the name, suitable for framing,
    and hanging by the flag on its pedestal, and the
        portrait in which he is forever young.

The flowered wreaths soon fade, but not the memories
    stored in The Wall, designed by a young Amerasian
        woman, to heal a riven nation.

Web of Circumstance

I have read that a spider's web
    has enormous tensile strength.

What I know from experience is
    that it's damned hard to let go of;

And I suspect that the spider's catch
    soon knows it's inescapable.

The metaphor of someone "trapped in a web"
    has a long thread of truth:

Tell a little social fib—Remember exactly how
    you dissembled—Repeat as needed—

Embellish as the need progresses—

Am I that fly in the spider's web?

Where's the Warranty? And Have You Read It?

Why is it that the wedding gift lamps thought to be
    solid brass are now rusting?
Why is it The Chef's cassoulet bubbling over and
    fouling the oven is charming, while mine doing
        exactly the same is just short of disgusting?

Why is it the neighbor's geraniums are relentlessly
    blooming splendid
When mine, soon after leaving the greenhouse,
    manage their short lives to be ended?

The parson's pet poodle is ever pious, never barking
    at strangers,
While my darling dachshund chases everyone, even
    across the street, oblivious of all dangers.

Now I, when making selections, always give the tedious
    process careful thought
As to whether the red, or the pink geraniums, to be planted
    next to the fuchsia, or the white impatiens, should be bought.

Having admired them in the shopping mall's parking lot,
    flourishing in high levels of carbon monoxide from the
        automobiles, fluorocarbons from hair spray at the beauty
        parlor, interacting with overheated oil fumes from

continued

THE GREASY SPOON, and throughout the summer
        temperatures quite hot—

Yes, flourishing where such deadly pollutants abound,
    yet mine, most tenderly yearned over on a breeze-
        blown hilltop, nevertheless curl up their new leaves,
          and fall down.

The puppy, chosen for traits vouchsafed by
    The American Kennel Club to result in the
        perfect home companion,
Soon suffers from an hereditary weakness of
    the spine, and requires his hind legs to be held up
        in a sling, just for simple perambulation.

Furthermore, and in conclusion,
    being unable to comprehend this confusion,

I tell you it's not just plants and pets that cause me
    problems; it's also appliances and automobiles
        and houses;

And far beyond that, most importantly, forever,
    until death parting,
        it's

    SPOUSES!!!

Widows and Orphans Are Fair Game

I've been scammed, flimflammed,
    and double damned
        more than once.

How could I have been so dumb
    as to let them come,
        such a dunce?

Perhaps because each scammer,
    and every flimflammer
        showed up at my door

Wearing a different hat,
    or some with no hat,
        but lies by the score.

I showed them smiles and good manners;
    should have been nails and hammers,
        and never a penny.

Should have had a broom in hand,
    and told every scheming man,
        "The lady of the house ain't in;

continued

"I'm the cleaning lady; I work here;"
　　and I doubt if they would dare
　　　to spout their spiel.

Then I could have closed the door,
　　walked away from the bore,
　　　showing only my heel.

Appendix

Blossoming

Ad Lib.

It ap-proach-es min-ute by min-ute the ho - ur___ When in-ci-pi-ent blos - soms shall flow-er.___ Oh, ho-ly,___ ho - ly,___ ho - - - ly,___ I am most whol - ly in-volved.___

mp

Slowly, evenly, simply

molto legato throughout

I care that spring shall a - gain e - rupt,
So that our spir - its, bank - rupt from win - ter's harsh with-
draw-als, Shall have the cash de - pos-its of love,
hope, com - mis - er - a - tion, And all know - ledge true Shall

flow be - tween me and you.

Hap - py,____ oh, most glo - rious spring-time, Rise up in us

all.____

Hap - py,＿＿＿＿ oh, most glo - rious spring - time,

Rise up in us all! Oh,
108
Ad Lib.
ho - ly, ho - ly, ho - - - ly, I am most
114
Slowly, evenly, simply
whol - ly in - volved.
119
8va
15ma
poco ritard.
124

Neither in youth, middle age, nor in my later years have I given much thought as to what I would be doing in old age. My philosophy has always been to deal with what is, both the good and the bad, and make of it the best I could.

It's been a long journey—I was born in Northern Virginia on April 1, 1918, and lived there for twenty-eight years, followed by twenty-two years in Southern Maryland; then in 1968, I moved to Chapel Hill, North Carolina, where I still live.

Needing to strike a balance between the required and the optional, I turned, more and more, to poetry, which has brought me to this collection, *Sundries*. In this volume I deal with both positives and negatives (or as we Unitarian Universalists say, "joys and concerns"). I hope you will find it worthwhile.

—Mitchell Forrest Lyman